The Truth About Catalogers

Other Books by Will Manley

Snowballs in the Bookdrop (1982)
Unintellectual Freedoms (McFarland, 1991)
Unprofessional Behavior (McFarland, 1992)
Unsolicited Advice (McFarland, 1992)
For Library Directors Only/For Library Trustees Only
(McFarland, 1993)
The Manley Art of Librarianship (McFarland, 1993)
Uncensored Thoughts (McFarland, 1994)

Other Books by Richard Lee

*You Can Tell Your Kid Will Grow Up to Be a
Librarian When . . .* (McFarland, 1992)

The Truth About Catalogers

by WILL MANLEY

Illustrations by
RICHARD LEE

with a foreword by
PHREDERICK JEWETT TUTTLE

McFarland & Company, Inc., Publishers
Jefferson, North Carolina, and London

British Library Cataloguing-in-Publication data are available

Library of Congress Cataloguing-in-Publication Data

Manley, Will, 1949–
    The truth about catalogers / by Will Manley : illustrations
by Richard Lee.
      p.   cm.
    Includes index.
    ISBN 0-7864-0103-6 (sewn softcover : 55# alk. paper) ∞
    1. Cataloging—United States. I. Title.
Z693.5.U6M35 1995
025.3—dc20   95-14828
                                          CIP

Manufactured in the United States of America

McFarland & Company, Inc., Publishers
 Box 611, Jefferson, North Carolina 28640

In memory of
Dr. Phrederick Jewett Tuttle
(1932–1994)

Acknowledgments

A book such as this which attempts to comprehensively cover the alpha and omega of Anglo-American cataloging could not even be attempted without the help and consultation of library science scholars too numerous to mention. It would, however, be remiss of me not to cite those special individuals who spent literally hundreds of hours with me in the preparation and editing of this text.

First and foremost I am indebted to Doctor Wally Friddle, Distinguished Fellow at the Eggington Information Studies Institute in Washington, D.C. Dr. Friddle was especially generous of his time and expertise in discussing the use of free floating subdivisions in creating subject headings for monographs dealing with bondage and bestiality.

Credit too should go to Professor Edweena Gorham-Hackstadt of the School of Library Studies at Minnesota State University. Her assistance in the area of hypens and dashes was simply invaluable. Also it would be an injustice not to mention the unconventional wisdom and solid judgment offered me by my colleague Virgil Gunther, director of cataloging services for the Gravel Point Public Library. Virgil's perspectives on colon abuse in on-line cataloging were highly instructive. And finally the material presented on the history of cataloging would have been far sketchier (and more boring!) without the assistance of Miss Zelda Goodykoontz, a Los Angeles psychic specializing in dead catalogers. Without her intervention my interviews with Melvil Dewey, Gertrude Mustard Strong, and Charles Ammi Cutter would have been impossible. Thanks, Zelda!

In view of the participation of these scholars I would like to point out that any errors or misinformation in this book should be attributed solely to them and not to me.

A Note About
the Illustrator

Richard Lee is the rarest of librarian/cartoonists. Not only is he a frequent contributor to such trade publications as *American Libraries* and the *Wilson Library Bulletin*, but his work has also appeared in such mainstream magazines as *Saturday Evening Post, Women's Day, Redbook, Biker World*, and *Velvet* (yes, *Velvet*).

For his day job he directs the Summerlin Branch of the Las Vegas/Clark County Library system. His hobbies include sending e-mail messages to Jamie Lee Curtis and cataloging fitness videos by Cindy Crawford. He received his M.L.S. from Brigham Young University (yes, Brigham Young) where he managed to get a C + and a B – in his two required cataloging courses.

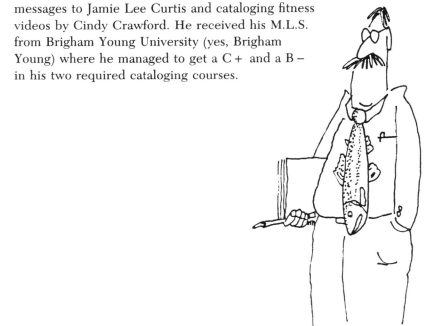

Table of Contents

Foreword

It is, of course, a matter of great pride, when one's student (especially a student one never thought really grasped the concepts of Anglo-American cataloging) writes a book about the subject that one taught him/her. In my forty year career as a professor of cataloging (distinguished professor for the past three years) at the Brookington Institute's Department of Library Studies, not one of my thousands of cataloging students ever wrote a book on any aspect of cataloging until Mr. Manley delivered this pithy gem to the literature of our worthy profession. It is rather like getting one's wife pregnant after many years of trying and hoping against hope.

Yes, this is a miracle, and one that I shall always treasure. I feel my career has crescendoed into a fitting climax, and so as the Brookington Institute phases out its library science department and forces me into a premature retirement, I take heart that my labors have born fruit. It's ironic, isn't it, that just when the administrative automatons who run this institution decide that there is no place for traditional library studies in the information age, one of its favorite sons produces a well researched and thoroughly convincing tome reaffirming the value of books and catalogers!

A word about Mr. Manley. As a student his young and inquisitive mind alternated between brilliance and buffoonery. At the time I will admit I thought the buffoon in Will dominated the brilliance (especially when he secretly poured a bottle of Bailey's Irish Cream into the faculty room coffee pot!) but now I can see that Will's buffoonery was simply an act he affected to shield himself from the social stigma that attaches to being a genius in a superficial culture. This I suppose is not surprising.

What is surprising, however, is Will's affinity for cataloging. One cannot read these pages without coming away with the sense that Will's love for the art of Anglo-American cataloging is quite real, and that his gentle teasing of its practitioners is a sign of endearment. Could it be? Is Will Manley a cataloger at heart? Is he one of us? Anyone who reads this book cannot think no.

September 24, 1994
    Phrederick Jewett Tuttle, D.L.S.
    Brookington Institute Department of Library Studies
    (defunct)

(Publisher's Note: Three days after writing this foreword Dr. Tuttle died in his den from a massive heart attack. Donations should be sent to the Missing Catalogers' Relief Fund.)

Preface
"A WORD OF CAUTION"

Not all of my writings about cataloging have been embraced with great enthusiasm by all catalogers. Just last year in the letters to the editor section of *American Libraries* I was excoriated for my "obnoxious and utterly uncalled for" comments about catalogers. In that same issue (September 1994) I was also attacked for reinforcing negative stereotypes about catalogers.

A general and objective review of everything I have written about catalogers over the past twenty years, however, reveals that I have a great deal of respect for the absolutely indispensible work they perform in developing bibliographic tools that connect readers with resources, and if I like to tease catalogers about their origins and destiny, well, that's simply a sign of endearment that most catalogers cheerfully tolerate and in some cases even enjoy.

In fact, contrary to their stern and humorless stereotypes, catalogers actually have great senses of humor. Unlike reference librarians and library directors they, in most cases, do not take themselves too seriously. Most of them know that by protesting their serious image they would simply reinforce it anyway. Therefore, more than other types of librarians, they have perfected the art of laughing at themselves.

For example, two years ago I did my standard library stand-up comedy act to the South Carolina Library Association. Included in the act was a series of jokes about catalogers (as well as every other type of librarian). After my presentation, a cataloger came up to me in anger and said, "I am furious with you."

"Which joke offended you?" I asked.

"I was offended because you didn't tell any jokes about serials catalogers. I feel completely neglected."

In this book, I've tried not to neglect any type of cataloger, and those of you who are uptight about your image, relax. In my next book I'll be going after reference librarians and then directors. When it comes to library commentary, I'm an affirmative action, equal opportunity guy.

Will Manley
January 1995

Introduction

I got the idea for this book from a letter that a cataloger from Illinois sent me not too long ago. In this letter (which she sent in response to something I had written about catalogers) she writes:

Dear Will,

CATALOGERS ARE PEOPLE TOO. I have noticed that while you show a great deal of respect for the work that we catalogers do, what with all the nitpicking our calling requires, you still find us to be a strange breed. I guess we are born with a certain mind-set that allows hierarchies of punctuation (when a colon is preferred over a semi-colon, and all that) to become beautiful architectures of logic and intellectual design. I love seminars on the new integrated MARC format, with the chance to discuss the nuances of when to add an 008 field and how to accommodate general material descriptors for multi-media materials, and a 740 field with proper indicators jumps out at me like an earth shattering sonic boom.

I can wax poetic on how to tell if something belongs to that esoteric category of realia. I was just born to be a cataloger. Maybe scientists will discover the gene that causes this malady. Most of our library world colleagues don't know how to react to us. While most people suspect that the librarians who win big on Jeopardy are reference librarians, I contend that most are probably catalogers, because we have to learn so many subtleties in the various subjects we catalog, to get the headings exactly right.

Ah, those Library of Congress subject headings... Only catalogers could bemoan the loss of "Addresses, essays, lectures" as a free-floating subdivision, even though we are in agreement that it never meant anything in the first place—it just added that air of scholarly officiousness to the subject headings tracings on the catalog card. Here's an interesting topic for debate: Is the concept of "May subdivide geographically" subversive? It encourages disunity and incites nationalism and localism at the expense of a common good.

In summary, maybe we catalogers are the spice of librarianship, adding the sort of flavor you find when you read about some of the mystic saints of the Middle Ages.

Sincerely,
(Name withheld)

For the past fifteen years I have received literally thousands of letters in response to my books and magazine columns. None, however, has been as thought provoking to me as this one. Let's be honest. You know as well as I do that for years in the library profession there have been whispers, rumors, suggestions, and even outright accusations that catalogers are somehow different than the rest of us, and while many of these rumors (catalogers are aliens, angels, demons, gremlins, etc.) seem to be the type of thing that generally originates in the *National Enquirer*, I for one have never entirely dismissed these theories out of hand.

It's quite riveting, therefore, to reflect upon the words of my cataloger pen pal. She seems quite directly ("I was just born to be a cataloger. Maybe scientists will discover the gene that causes this malady") to affirm the basic assumption that CATALOGERS ARE INTRINSICALLY DIFFERENT. Thus while only Nixon could go to China, it follows logically that only a cataloger could reveal that only a certain, select few have the intrinsic quality of catalogerness.

This, of course, brings us to the essential purpose of this book—which is to examine in depth the origin and nature of this special quality of catalogerness.

Chapter 1

THEORIES ON
THE ORIGIN
OF CATALOGERS

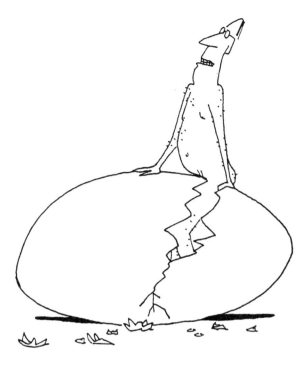

The origin of catalogers is a mystery that over the ages has challenged archeologists, astronomers, and theologians. In general there have been a diversity of explanations based upon three foundational theories:

1) interplanetary visitation

2) divine intervention, and

3) biological evolution.

MAIN ENTRY THEORY

This theory, first advanced by Dr. Heinrich Wilhelm von Frinke in his groundbreaking work, *Aliens Among Us*, suggests that sometime in the period between 3000 and 2500 B.C., a large spaceship from a distant planet in the Andromeda galaxy deposited 50,000 cataloger/aliens into an obscure South Pacific island named Realia. Forced to leave their home planet because of a nuclear war that was triggered by a dispute about whether authors should be listed by real name or pseudonym, these aliens gradually adapted to earth conditions and fanned out all over the globe. The evidence for this theory is the existence of large stone sculptures on Realia that look like catalogers. Scientists say these sculptures date back to 2000 B.C.

FIRST ADDED ENTRY THEORY

Building upon von Frinke's theory, Dr. Maurice Legrande of the Sorbonne suggests in his book, *Visitors from Afar*, that although the catalogers' planet of origin was rocked by a nuclear war, it was not destroyed, and in the 16th century A.D. a second spaceship arrived with 5,000 additional cataloger/aliens. This new influx came to help existing catalogers get bibliographic control of the proliferation of books and printed materials brought on by the invention of the printing press.

SECOND ADDED ENTRY THEORY

According to Orville E. Fleckinger, a former N.A.S.A. engineer, there is intriguing evidence that a second added entry of alien/catalogers took place in 1993. In his book *What Your Government Does Not Want You to Know About Outer Space*, Fleckinger indicates that shortly after N.A.S.A. lost communication with the Mars probe it received a series of random radio signals in M.A.R.C. format. What was most puzzling about these messages was that the signal 025.3 kept appearing. Recognizing this as the Dewey Decimal number for cataloging, Fleckinger hypothesizes that these signals were transmitted by a new group of alien/catalogers who apparently came to earth to help their early colleagues bring order to the chaos resulting from the explosion of electronic data.

THE SURVIVORS
OF ATLANTIS THEORY

In June of 1989 while searching for the remains of the Lusitania, underwater archeologist Gerhardt Olberding accidently happened upon the ruins of what appears to have been a highly developed city/state that sank beneath the sea after a violent earthquake. In an article in *The Journal of Oceanic Archeology*, Olberding argues that these ruins are probably from the legendary Greek colony of Atlantis, which he suggests may have been settled by catalogers because he found the following building inscriptions — "Store, General"; "Clinic, Medical"; and "Library, Public." Olberding believes that those who survived the catastrophe settled in Europe and took their cataloging art with them.

THE LOST TRIBES
OF ISRAEL THEORY

In his doctoral dissertation, *A Literary Search for the Ten Lost Tribes of Israel*, Rabbi Moshe Lendelbaum through an exhaustive process of textual deconstruction reveals that *AACR2* bears an uncanny resemblance in tone, format, and message to the *Book of Deuteronomy*. In his concluding sentence Rabbi Lendelbaum writes, "*AACR2* could only have been written by scribes from the ten lost tribes of Israel that were scattered by the four winds after Assyria defeated Israel in 731 B.C."

DIVINE INTERVENTION THEORY

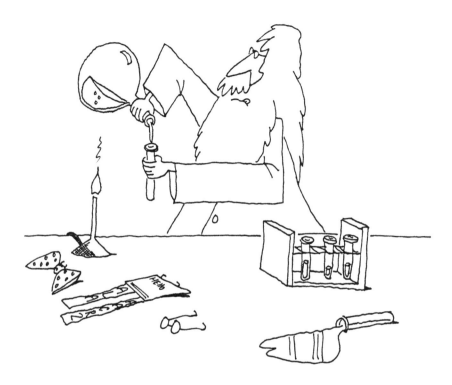

Father Philip Freneau, S.J., a strong proponent of intervention theology, writes in his book *God Is Not an Absentee Landlord* that "God so loves the world that he not only sent his only son, Jesus Christ, but that he continuously sends us special people to help us handle special tasks." Among the special people God has created and sent us are V.C.R. repairmen, stand-up comedians, and catalogers. Freneau bases his argument on the fact that God, HIMSELF, loves to catalog and classify as shown in the first few chapters of Genesis. "God in a sense," writes Freneau, "was the First Cataloger."

THE ANGEL THEORY

    In his book *Angels on Earth*, Edwin Hopkins, a reference librarian and self proclaimed angelologist relates a story about the time that he and a cataloger named Maude R. were traveling to an A.L.A. conference together on a 747 from Omaha, Nebraska, to Chicago. The plane was hit by a bolt of lightning that knocked out its engines. While the plane was in rapid descent Maude grabbed Edwin and hurried out the emergency door. They floated gently down to earth and were the only survivors. "I swear I could feel the beating of wings on Maude's back," wrote Edwin.

THE GRAND UNIFIED THEORY
(G.U.T.)

In his masterwork, *God's Creations*, Dr. E. Stringfellow Barrow, Professor of Deity Studies at the Ockham School of Theology, has shaped the preceding eight theories into a kind of synthesis which he calls his "Grand Unified Theory." Dr. Barrow writes, "The ages-long mystery about the origin of catalogers can be solved by looking at all the disparate pieces of evidence that anthropologists, archeologists, and theologians have uncovered about catalogers over the last 1800 years and fitting them together to create one unified theory." According to Barrow, God sensed the need to tidy his creation up a bit and so he created a race of angelic catalogers on an unnamed Andromeda galaxy planet. These cataloger/angels came to earth on three different occasions to cope with the challenges brought on by the development of new information technologies. These alien beings first migrated from the South Seas to Israel to Atlantis and now occupy every corner of the earth.

THE CLEAR AS MUD THEORY

Dr. Wilbert S. Grob, in his *History of Mud*, says that all the planetary and theological interventionist theories are ridiculous nonsense that have been created by con-artists, frauds, and flim flam men. There is nothing mystical about catalogers. Sure, they are a little weird, but that doesn't mean that they are space men or angels anymore than the dodo bird was sent to earth on a special mission to make people laugh. The simple truth is that like everything else under the sun, catalogers evolved naturally from mud.

Chapter 2

CATALOGERS AND SEX

Perhaps it is because of the prevalence of the theory that catalogers are extraterrestrial beings that an image has developed around catalogers that stereotypes them as quiet, serious, and sexless beings who procreate in some weird celibate fashion. There is, of course, an unfair prejudice involved in this portrayal. There is absolutely no scientific evidence to suggest that extraterrestrial beings do not engage in the physical enjoyments of the procreative act. Furthermore the sex survey that I conducted of the library profession indicated that catalogers do indeed have a strong physical attraction for each other and that they do consummate these desires in the normal diversity of positions and locations. What may be considered a bit unusual is their admitted preference for conducting their intimacies in hotel elevators but this is easily explained by the fact that at library conferences catalogers (perhaps because of their low pay) tend to double and triple up in hotel rooms, and thus the elevator becomes a rare venue of privacy in the late evening hours.

Fred, I know there's no C.I.P. information in the Madonna book but really how many days does it take to catalog one book?

"My orientation? I swing either way—L.C. or Dewey."

Hey, babe, he may like to brag about his main entries but if you come home with me I'll show you some really creative added entries.

My sexual history? Well, ten years ago I cataloged *The Joy of Sex*, five years ago I contributed the first M.A.R.C. record to O.C.L.C. for *The Hite Report*, and last year I wrote an article for *Cataloging Hotline* on how to catalog Madonna's *Sex*. Other than that I'm perfectly clean.

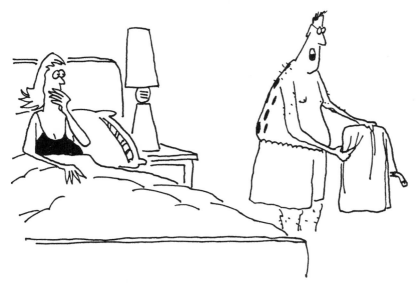

Those spots on my body? That's just Dutch elm disease. Last Arbor Day I kind of got involved with an elm tree.

Oh, Harold, I love it when you talk Dewey to me.

Chapter 3

THE ROLE THAT CATALOGING HAS PLAYED IN WORLD HISTORY

One of the biggest misconceptions about cataloging is that in the circus of life it is a mere sideshow, and that the main events of history have taken place in the arenas of religion, government, technology, law, and economics. The conventional wisdom is that cataloging is a mere handmaiden to these big, important professions. According to Dr. Mortimer Hopwood, however, nothing could be farther from the truth. In his book, *The Truth About World History*, he writes, "Anyone who accepts at face value the 'facts' presented in standard history textbooks is living a life of blissful ignorance." Dr. Hopwood spent his entire professional career investigating many of the biggest and most famous events in history and his research revealed over 3,500 serious factual errors. Of these thousands of errors ten involved how cataloging has helped shape the world as we know it today from the creation of the universe to the twentieth century.

GOD CREATES THE UNIVERSE FROM THE L.C. LIST OF SUBJECT HEADINGS

It's right there in the Book of John — "In the beginning was the Word and the Word was with God." Theologians, of course, have debated endlessly over the meaning of the word, "Word." Hopwood's theory (*The Truth About the Origin of the Universe*) is that the word is the Library of Congress List of Subject Headings, which he says existed before the beginning of time and will exist after the end of time. He writes, "With the possible exception of the Sears Catalog, no document covers the totality of God's creation with the comprehensiveness of the L.C. subject headings." It was obviously the recipe book that God used to cook up His/Her universe. Could that be why whenever renegade catalogers attack the list for being racist, sexist, or out-of-date, the folks at the Library of Congress simply smile and say very smugly, "The List has been around for a long, long time and will be around for an even longer time."

PLATO ATTEMPTS TO DEFINE REALIA

Plato is commonly seen as the father of modern philosophy. Supposedly he's the guy who started us thinking about the distinctions between reality and illusion. All of Western thought is founded upon his writings. Unfortunately, experts on ancient Greek culture now feel that Plato's works were mistranslated. It turns out that Plato was not concerned with reality. He was concerned with realia. More specifically he was interested in the difference between realia and artefacts. More astounding is the discovery that Plato was not a philosopher after all, but rather a cataloger who was trying to write a set of rules and regulations that would standardize the bibiographic records of ancient Greece. Plato's brilliance is shown by the fact that his writings on the realia/artefact duality pre-date *AACR2*'s treatment of the issue by 3,000 years.

KING ARTHUR FORMS
THE CATALOGERS OF
THE ROUND TABLE

The story is all very wonderful. Arthur, Merlyn, Guinevere, and Launcelot had a dream to bring the order of law to a chaotic world. They called their dream Camelot. What's wrong with this picture? It's totally false, that's what. The truth is that under Merlyn's tutelage, Arthur became something of a bookworm. The more he read, the more he became frustrated. His own court library was limited and the concept of interlibrary loan was simply impossible because of the chaotic nature of the bibliographic records being kept. Arthur decided to change all that. He wanted to bring the order of cataloging law to this chaos. He therefore summoned the finest catalogers from all over the literate world and formed them into his Catalogers of the Round Table. Oh, one last thing. Arthur never named his kingdom Camelot; he called it Catelog.

WILLIAM TELL SHOOTS
THE FIRST ON-LINE CATALOG

It is hard to think of an historical event that has been more cele-brated on stage and in song than the story of William Tell. The problem is that everyone from Schiller to Rossini has gotten the story wrong. Yes, Tell, an ardent young idealist rebelled against tyrannical authority and yes, Gessler, his cruel oppresser, made him shoot an apple off his young son's head. But here's the rest of the story. Tell was actually a very in-novative cataloger at the local university where he perfected the first COMCAT which was shaped like an apple (hence Apple computers, stupid). Gessler, the anti-technology director of the library, was incensed at Tell for wasting work time on his "contraption." The ultimatum Gess-ler gave him was a simple one: Shoot your kid or your computer.

SIR ISAAC NEWTON ORIGINATES
THE AUTHOR, TITLE, SUBJECT
ACCESS POINTS

With the possible exception of the apple that William Tell shot off his son's head, there can't be a more famous piece of fruit in the annals of history than the apple that plunked Sir Isaac Newton on the head and made him think of the law of gravity. Actually, the truth is that there were three apples that fell on Newton, one right after the other, and the epiphany he experienced was not the law of gravity (he discovered that later under a pear tree) but the law of triple access—author, title, and subject. You see, Sir Isaac's day job was science cataloger for the British Museum, and for years he had been struggling for a way to create a better bibliographic access for the library's patrons. Thank God for apples.

KING RICHARD III KILLS COURT
CATALOGER'S NEW LIST
OF SUBJECT HEADINGS

"Off with his head!" is a famous quote from history. Shakespeare and Lewis Carroll are among the many authors who have stolen it. Who was the first to use it? Was it King Henry V? No, stupid, he's the one who said "Off with HER head!" Was it Marie Antoinette? No, she's the one who said, "Let them eat cake." Actually it was King Richard III. Remember him? He was the King of England from 1483 to 1485. But let's set the record straight about one thing—he never said "Off with his head." What he actually said was, "Off with his headings." Yes, that's right—nothing could ignite King Richard's considerable temper like bad cataloging, and when the Court Cataloger presented his majesty with a new list of subject headings, Richard was not pleased. Can you believe that one of the new headings was—"Kings of England—Drunks, Thieves, and Rapists"? The hapless cataloger was very fortunate, indeed, to keep his own head intact.

KARL MARX CALLS CATALOGERS
TO ACTION

Everyone knows that Karl Marx originated the theory of communism. But Marx, contrary to public opinion, was himself not a flame-throwing revolutionary. He was a quiet and reserved bookworm, who preferred the peace and quiet of an academic library to the noise and tumult of the streets. Throughout his lifetime of quiet research and study, Marx noticed how oppressed catalogers seemed to be. He felt they were always stuck in unhealthy workrooms devoid of light and heat. "Their masters seem to think that they are mushrooms who will prosper in cool, dark rooms," Marx is reported to have said about catalogers. He also objected to their long hours, low pay, and lack of professional respect. Marx's *Communist Manifesto* was originally entitled *Catalogers' Manifesto*, but was later changed by his sidekick, Friedrich Engels, to reflect a more universal concern with the plight of the proletariat.

LENIN ATTACKS
AUTHORITY CONTROL

   "QUESTION AUTHORITY" is a bumper sticker that came into vogue during the turbulent 1960s. Research reveals, however, that the phrase may well have originated in the early writings of Vladimir Ilyich Lenin, the Russian revolutionary. Lenin, the son of a Volga library inspector, was an idealistic young man who went to library school and was shocked by the abuse meted out by a misanthropic cataloging professor who spanked students with a card catalog rod when they made a mistake involving authority control. The once mild mannered Lenin became a bibliographic anarchist. In his master's thesis, which was entitled "Question Authority Control," Lenin opposed all forms of authority control as being autocratic and arbitrary. As a footnote it should also be clarified that Lenin never intended to found the Union of Soviet Socialist Republics. What he really set out to accomplish was to start a Union list of Soviet Socialist serials, but things got out of control in 1917 and the Soviet empire was formed instead.

HITLER BURNS
CATALOGING TREATISES

    The famous Nazi book burnings of 1933 should have given the world a wake-up call about the true intentions of the German Nazi Party, but the world sat back and closed its eyes while thousands of books written by Jews, Bolsheviks, catalogers, and other disruptive dissidents were burned. Did I say catalogers? Yes I did. It's not something that you will read in most history books, but every cataloging treatise in the library of the University of Berlin was burned to ashes on the night of May 10, 1933. Why were these books targeted? Did Hitler hate catalogers? No, but Hitler did hate libraries. He saw them as a threat to his propaganda machine, and he knew that at the heart of librarianship is the catalog. If Hitler could destroy the practice of cataloging, he knew he could render libraries useless.

Chapter 4

CATALOGERS ON THE INFORMATION SUPERHIGHWAY

More than any other type of librarian the cataloger has been impacted by the advent of computer technology. Not only have catalogers had to phase out the manual card catalogs that they slaved over for so many years, but they have also been expected to design perfect on-line catalogs that will satisfy the sophisticated information needs of an increasingly computer literate society. While many library observers feel that large centralized bibliographic networks like O.C.L.C. and R.L.I.N. will eliminate the need for professional catalogers at local libraries, the truth is that like taxes, lint, and death, the cataloger will always be with us. Traveling on this new superhighway, however, as the following pages show, will be quite a challenge!

Fred's our on-line cataloger. He's been wearing that ever since the system crashed last week.

No, Harold when I asked you to implement a voice mail system, I didn't mean a mailbox tied to a radio.

Sometimes I feel like roadkill on the information superhighway.

Ted is our virtual cataloger.

Emma always buckles up before heading out on to the fast lane.

Chapter 5

DEAD CARD CATALOGS AND DEAD CATALOGERS

The most obvious manifestation of the computer age in libraries would of course be the appearance of computer catalogs and the disappearance of card catalogs. To many observers it was quite surprising to see the glee with which catalogers abandoned their manual catalogs. You would have thought more tears would have been shed. After all, these old catalogs were the product of decades and even centuries of painstaking work, and many of them were impressive resources of scholarship and erudition. But all through the '70s, '80s, and '90s, catalogers abandoned them with the same kind of gleeful enthusiasm that one gets rid of an old car that is in a constant state of disrepair. For example the cataloging department of the Maryland Health Sciences Library put out a whimsical little publication entitled "101 Uses for a Dead Catalog Card," in which it was suggested that catalog cards could be used as tablecloth crumb scrapers, fish scalers, jousting targets, and cat litter. With the same sort of gallows humor we felt it fair play to suggest the following uses of dead catalogers.

Scarecrow to keep flies off library staff barbecue

Paper holder

Lawn Sculpture

Library Security Guard

Door Stopper

Coffee Table

Prop for Halloween Story Hour

Coat Hanger

Car Companion that allows you to drive in car-pool lane

Projection Screen Holder

Chapter 6

CONTEMPORARY CATALOGING ISSUES

At what age did you first start to worry about the distinction between a dash and a hyphen?

Generally when we talk about the hot issues of cataloging we talk about things like the future of the main entry, the feasibility of developing one integrated international bibliographic network, and the problems involved with cataloging new media formats. Since these hot button issues are covered very comprehensively in other publications, I have decided to concentrate my focus on some current issues that have not received as much professional attention. The fact that these issues do not deal with the technicalities and conundrums of everyday cataloging, however, does not mean that they are not important. As we have stated previously, catalogers are a tightly bonded and misunderstood group. Understanding some of their more personal issues can only result in a closer collegiality with the rest of the profession.

THE FUTURE OF CATALOGING 101

The biggest issue in contemporary cataloging is whether Cataloging 101 should continue to be a required course for all library school students. Many experts feel that cataloging has become so automated that the average library school student will never be called upon in the course of a forty year career to ever catalog a book. On the other side of the issue is Dr. Hartenstein A. Segue, who in an article entitled "Taking Cataloging 101 Is as Important as Wearing Undergarments" lists four basic reasons why cataloging should continue to be required:

1) Required cataloging courses keep cataloging professors busy, and hordes of unemployed cataloging professors would be a menace to society;

2) Required cataloging courses keep normal people out of the library profession and this is important because normal people would not work nights and weekends for peanuts;

3) The misery of required cataloging courses provides a good bonding experience for library school students; and

4) Eliminating required cataloging courses would not be fair to the thousands of suckers who have suffered through them in the past.

CATALOGER CRIMES

A recent crime study released by the F.B.I. reveals that the crimes most frequently committed by catalogers are the following:

1) Parking in handicapped spaces

2) Throwing washers into toll booth baskets

3) Driving in the car pool lane with an inflatable doll of Charles Ammi Cutter as front seat companion

4) Faking knee injuries so as to be able to pre-board airplanes alongside the physically challenged and mothers of small children

5) Murdering reference librarians who constantly ask that "books be re-cataloged to conform to local practices"

6) Assaulting street mimes who refuse to give directions at A.L.A. conferences

7) Secretly re-arranging library periodical collections by fragrance

8) Blowing a high frequency whistle outside the fence at the local dog pound

9) Sneaking into Disney World in a mouse suit

10) Sticking a ticking alarm clock in the top drawer of the reference desk and then calling in a bomb threat.

CATALOGER PRANKS

Anyone who thinks that catalogers don't have a sense of humor has never been victimized by a cataloger prank. In his book, *Librarians Have More Fun*, R. Rosewell Gidry gives a list of pranks that catalogers have played on him and other unsuspecting librarians:

1) Talking to imaginary friends during library staff meetings

2) Sucking yogurt through a straw in staff lounge in front of reference librarians who are trying to eat lunch

3) Flossing teeth while driving staff van

4) Changing all catalog entries for Richard Nixon to "Tricky Dick"

5) Secretly putting a "Shit Happens" bumper sticker on the library's bookmobile

6) Putting a baby piranha in the children's room fish tank

7) Putting live cockroaches in the reference desk drawer

8) Hiding in the bookdrop and saying "thank you" every time someone deposits a book

9) Putting a plate of marijuana brownies in the staff lounge.

WHAT CATALOGERS WATCH ON T.V.

Recent Nielsen findings reveal that the T.V. programs most watched by catalogers are:

1) C-Span live at the Original Cataloging Department of the Library of Congress

2) 24 Hour Ice Fishing Channel

3) National Bingo Championship live from Sun City

4) Library Science Dissertation Defense Channel

5) P.B.S. Nature Series: In Search of Earthworms

6) P.B.S. Health Series: You and Your Spleen

7) The People's Overdue Fine Court

8) 24 Hour Senior Shuffleboard League in Sun City

9) The American Sportsman Roadkill Series

10) America's Funniest Cataloging Bloopers

11) Wide World of Sports Special on Donkeys Parachuting Out of Airplanes

12) Cow Racing at Churchill Downs

13) Current Events Discussion with Marcel Marceau

14) Winnebago Racing from the Daytona Speedway

15) The Weed Wacker Olympics.

AFFINITY FOR CATS

In a recent survey on the subject of Librarians and Death, 72 percent of the catalogers who responded indicated that they would like to be reincarnated as cats. More startling, however, is the announcement at a recent American Veterinary Society convention that there is evidence that a number of catalogers have metamorphosed into cats in their lifetimes. The Society even issued a bulletin entitled "Warning Signs That Your Cataloger Is Turning Into a Cat." The following signs were listed:

1) Licks fingers before and after meals

2) Fish consumption increases

3) Begins wearing catsuits despite 87 percent body fat

4) Stops biting nails and starts growing them long and pointed

5) Spends afternoon coffee breaks napping under desk

6) Asks whether library's self insured medical program covers vet bills

7) Begins obsessing about the mouse that lives behind the coke machine in the staff lounge

8) During pregnancy uses the word litter instead of baby

9) Circulates petitions advocating dog leash laws

10) Strange bulge in the pants suggests growth of tail

11) Answers to "Here Pussy, Pussy"

12) Puts litter box in staff restroom.

CATALOGER MONEY TIPS

Yes, catalogers are frugal. They have to be! Have you seen what the going rate is for an ambidextrous, tri-lingual, multi-cultural cataloger — about $19,500. In an article for *Library World Weekly* entitled "How I Paid Off a Thirty Year Mortgage and Put a Kid Through Harvard," Howard Fergus Bottomley, cataloger for the Philopian Institute Library, gives the following money tips:

1) Save money on laundry by just turning underwear inside out every time you get dressed

2) Stand on freeway with WILL CATALOG FOR FOOD sign

3) Give your children refrigerator boxes for Christmas

4) Pose as a panhandler at A.L.A. Conferences and beg for "book" money

5) Roam under the bleachers with a metal detector after high school football games

6) Save on hot water bills by taking sponge baths in the library restroom

7) Include low fat, low cholesterol library paste in your daily diet

8) Take advantage of Goodwill's impressive selection of sans-a-belt pants

9) Wear pants with big pockets to library vendor hospitality suites so you can stock up on nuts and pretzels.

Chapter 7

A PEEK THROUGH THE CATALOGING ROOM KEYHOLE

Theories abound as to why catalogers are so reserved and serious. Some people explain their quietude as an occupational hazard. After all, what is the work of cataloging and classification but the difficult and painstaking process of reducing volumes of information down to a few terse subject headings. Catalogers, or so the theory goes, are therefore disciplined to be serious people of few words. I for one do not agree with this assessment. In my mind there are no livelier, funnier, more lovably eccentric beings in the universe than catalogers. They have gotten a bad rap for being quiet and severe because all too often they have been segregated unfairly into their own basement or backroom ghettoes far from the public services staff. Let's be honest, cataloging workrooms often tend to be architectural afterthoughts, but did you ever wonder what goes on in these rooms? Well, here's a peek.

We're from the county health department and we're here to check for a dirty database.

I need a vacation. Everything's beginning to look like a 333.33 to me.

You'd think that just once we'd get a great big coffee table book full of spontaneous photographs of catalogers cataloging.

Harold likes to think of himself as an original cataloger.

This is what happens when you use the wrong subject heading. Miss Mudge puts you in stocks.

Mr. Billikens, can you help me with this book? I don't know what subject headings to use. It's about loss, redemption, and fantastic sex.

Oliver, the next time you use a colon instead of a comma, I'm going to send you to Dr. Frederick and have you checked for colon abuse.

Zelda catalogs all our large print books.

Chapter 8

NETWORKING

Perhaps the biggest impact that computer technology has had on the discipline of cataloging is the trend toward networking. In fact, knowledgeable cataloging futurists boldly predict that sometime in the not too distant future all cataloging data will be centralized in one big international bibliographic network. Right now, it is common knowledge that there are three major national online bibliographic networks— O.C.L.C., R.L.N., and W.L.N.—and a diversity of regional networks like SOLINET and PALINET. What many people do not realize, however, is that catalogers have also cobbled together a number of small, special interest networks that give them an opportunity to get together on a regular basis to share common interests and activities. On the following pages for the first time we will reveal these "nets."

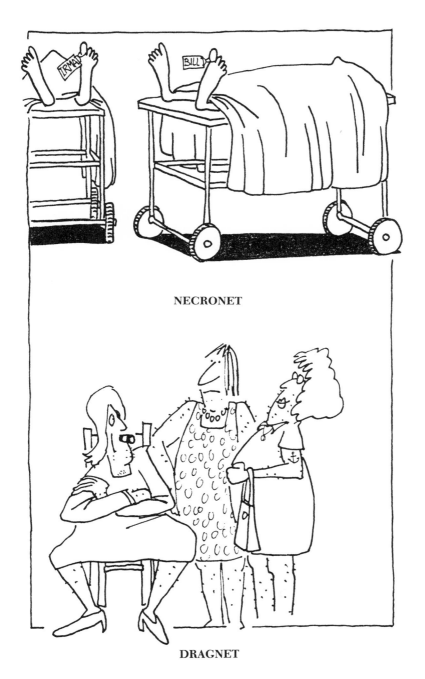

NECRONET

DRAGNET

NERFNET

HAIRNET

(W)HORNET

FISHNET

Chapter 9

THE ANGLO-AMERICAN CATALOGING HALL OF FAME

Perched in the sleepy English village of Knode (the place where Sir Isaac Newton was sitting under an apple tree and was hit in the head by three successive apples and shortly thereafter devised the author, title, and subject approach to cataloging) is the Cataloger's Hall of Fame and Theme Park. It's an instructive experience to walk through this museum and experience its various exhibits. The most popular attractions are the Isadora Mudge kissing booth, the audioanamatronic accession number lecture by Charles Ammi Cutter, the Melvil Dewey purple polka dot underwear exhibit, the authority control duel (two actors dressed up as Sam Clemens and Mark Twain engaging in a mock gunfight battle), and the Gertrude Mustard Strong cross dressing peep show.

Many people mistakenly think that the history of cataloging was dominated by hoary white bearded Victorian men and women who felt drinking was a sin, homosexuality a kind of insanity, and non-procreative sex a perversion. A stroll through the Cataloger's Hall of Fame, however, reveals that many notable catalogers led very colorful lives.

MURIEL LIVINGSTON FRUMP

Dr. Pauline Frump was the Irving C. Limberg Professor of Cataloging at Jefferson University from 1893 to 1924. A pioneer in the area of author control, she is best remembered for the quote: "In life you're entitled to one name and one name only." She strongly advocated that catalogers and not authors should determine main entry names. Frump dedicated her life to tracking down the real names of authors and is credited with founding a secret society, the C.I.A. (Catalogers' Investigation Association) which did background checks on all new authors to determine if they were using a pseudonym. Frump was also a strong advocate that legislation be passed to make it the use of a pseudonym punishable by decapitation.

FATHER PHILIP FEASLEY

Father Feasley was the ringleader of the "Dewey 9," a renegade band of catalogers from St. Elmo's College in Washington, D.C., who broke into libraries after midnight and poured goats' blood over catalog cards with the heading "Vietnam Conflict" to protest the use of the euphemistic word "Conflict" instead of the more honest term "War." He also urged all Americans to burn their library cards in protest to this subject heading. When the war ended Father Feasley began to wage guerrilla warfare against the Library of Congress for their use of what he called "sexist," "racist," and "imperialist" subject headings. When L.C. made the transformation to a computer catalog, Feasley, an amateur hacker, constantly broke into their system and arbitrarily erased subject headings he did not like.

H. WYNDHAM BARNWELL

Dr. H. Wyndham Barnwell, Professor of Dirtband Studies at the Dummermuth Institute in London from 1932 to 1959, is credited for developing the science of card catalog carbon dating and dirtbanding. Although this science is now defunct, dirtbanding was a recognized methodology that many libraries used to evaluate their collections and to acquire new books. By measuring and dating the streaks of dirt, grime, and wear on a series of catalog cards, Barnwell was able to determine what subject areas were in greatest demand. This cost effective alternative to keeping and tabulating detailed circulation records was widely used up until the early 1980s when many card catalogs were discarded.

ELVIRA FLEMM

Elvira Flemm was elected to the Cataloger's Hall of Fame for the highly innovative and creative card catalog that she developed at the Malibu Public Library. Flemm, an amateur painter of seascapes, was hired in the cataloging department for her exquisite penmanship. Shortly after being employed she began to realize the artistic possibilities for the catalog, and decided that with a few extra touches she could transform it into something quite tactile and sensory. For instance, she sprinkled salt water and sand on catalog cards dealing with the ocean and ocean life and whittled thin, wooden cards for books on woodworking and furniture making. Subject cards for needlework were bordered with fringe, and in the drawer containing the subject heading humor a three foot toy snake jumped out whenever you opened it.

MANFRED GORKY

Manfred Gorky was a Russian immigrant who came to the United States in 1905 shortly after the abortive Bolshevik revolt. So difficult did Gorky find the ordeal of learning a new language, that he became a strong advocate of the Esperanto movement. Esperanto was an international language introduced in 1887 by Dr. Ludwig Zamenhoff of Poland. After locating in Yellow Lake, Idaho, Gorky found work as the chief cataloger for Northwest State College Library where he converted the card catalog to Esperanto. Five weeks after the installation of the new catalog, Gorky was stabbed to death in the neck by a frustrated library patron wielding a steel card catalog rod. In the ensuing trial, the defendant pleaded not guilty by reason of insanity. "Esperanto," he said, "was making me crazy." The jury agreed and Gorky's killer was acquitted.

SIR EDMUND RIBBESDALE

Sir Ribbesdale was an academic cataloger who explored all forms of utopian thinking from anarchism to naturism and finally concluded that the only way to achieve a perfect society was by repopulating the world with catalogers. He, therefore, encouraged male catalogers to have as much sex as possible, but when he discovered that the average male cataloger has trouble finding one mate per lifetime let alone several, he founded a new magazine called *Stud* with the idea of glorifying the cataloging lifestyle. After two issues the magazine failed. Next, Ribbesdale tried to get catalogers excluded from polygamy laws and tried to get tax credits for women bearing cataloger children. After this flopped, Ribbesdale was arrested in a sperm bank where he was caught replacing the existing stock with cataloger sperm.

Chapter 10

CATALOGING ASSOCIATIONS

Is it because cataloging is essentially quiet, solitary work that catalogers absolutely love to form and join professional organizations? Or is it because cataloging is an exacting and complex science that requires the kind of collaboration that professional associations encourage and foster? Whatever the reason, catalogers are the most gregarious of librarians, and they seem to have a task force, round table, and committee for every issue, problem, and purpose. But we are mistaken if we think that catalogers do nothing but debate and discuss issues at library conferences. They also seem to love to gather together and socialize with their own. As one cataloger said to me, "When I'm with other catalogers I don't feel weird or alien." Ever wonder what catalogers chat about at their cocktail parties and conference get togethers? Well, recently I had the opportunity to eavesdrop and this is what I heard.

Phil, I'd like you to meet Mabel. She's doing some interesting things with semi-colons.

My wife doesn't understand me. I told her that I'm a cataloger and if she wanted more conversation she should have married Ted Koppel.

Don't look at your relationship with Bill as a marriage; look at it as a long running serial with updates.

In library school I experimented with flavored mineral waters. Now I think I'm ready to try some cherry wine coolers.

Hi, I'd like you to meet Phil. He's sort of the pocket part of my life.

Harold, don't you think you're taking your new job as a botanical cataloging specialist too seriously?

Chapter 11

A LIBRARY
LOVE STORY

One important issue that I investigated in my "American Libraries" survey was the mating habits of catalogers. It turns out that many catalogers (45%) do marry outside the tribe, but the fact remains that the other 55% prefer their own. "Only a cataloger can truly appreciate and love another cataloger" was a typical remark. "I could really only love someone who speaks my language" was another oft quoted comment. And "Only another cataloger could understand my need to index my compact disc collection" was a third observation that was repeated in several different variations. Do cataloger/cataloger marriages work? In a word "yes!" Cataloger unions tend to be characterized by caring, sharing, and hoping that the children will grow up to be catalogers!

Oh, Virgil, you don't look anything like your e-mail.

Olivia, the opera was very edifying but now it's time for some fun. How about you and I going back to my apartment to do a little boolean searching together.

Okay, Virgil, I'm ready to hyphenate. I'll be your wife.

Do you, Virgil, take this woman to be your wife for better or worse, in sickness and in health, through all editions of *AACR2*?

Virgil, wouldn't it be easier to just do this in vitro?

Olivia, there's nothing in *AACR2* about assigning main entries to babies. It looks like we're going to have to do some original cataloging.

For God's sakes, Olivia, little Nellie is only four months old. She'll have plenty of time to get into free floating subdivisions when she's older.

I'm sorry, Sally, but Nellie can't come out today. She's creating authority files for her horse books.

Virgil, I'm devastated. Nellie says she's decided to become a reference librarian. Where did we go wrong?

Now that Nellie is away at library school and we've got the house all to ourselves let's do something crazy like convert our library to Ranganathan.

Chapter 12

AN ILLUSTRATED GLOSSARY OF CATALOGING TERMS

Free Floating Subdivision

More than any other branch of librarianship, the discipline of cataloging has its own language and syntax. Unless you are a cataloger, for example, the terms, "free floating subdivision," "hanging indentation," "open system interconnection," "post-coordinate indexing," "scope note," "purposive analysis," "unity analysis," "collocation," and "coextensive subject entry" constitute a foreign language. This, of course, is one of the reasons why theories have surfaced in the library profession that catalogers originated on an alien celestial body. What follows is an illustrated glossary that will help the non-cataloger develop a better understanding of "catalogese."

Serial Catalogers

Main Entry and Added Entries

Joint Authors

Microfiche Catalogers

Authority Control

Serial Killers

Original Catalogers

Automated Cataloging

On-Line Cataloging

Retrospective Conversion

Chapter 13

IN SEARCH
OF CATALOGERS

After all the homework that I did for this book, I came to the unsettling conclusion that I still really didn't know catalogers, not completely anyway. Sure, it was interesting to uncover some of the little known historical facts about the profession and it was helpful to discover what other researchers had found out about them, but I still hadn't been able to put my finger on what makes the average cataloger tick. What is it that distinguishes catalogers from everyone else? What exactly is that very real but hard to define quality of catalogerness? I realized it was time for me to do some of my own original research, and so through the monthly column that I write for *American Libraries* I conducted a ten question survey, which 573 catalogers responded to. What follows are the results of that survey.

WHAT CATALOGERS LIKE ABOUT
BEING A CATALOGER

The universal bonding between catalogers, the beautiful logic of *AACR2*, giving order to chaos, the gratification of creating a tangible product, nights and weekends off, don't have to kowtow to the idiotic public, don't have to deal with perverts, the fact that non-catalogers don't understand cataloging and therefore leave us alone, the power to erase access points or delete records of books you do not like, caressing new books first, being able to eat, drink and listen to music while working, working with machines rather than people, the wonderful absurdity that corporate bodies can be considered authors, holding reference librarians and patrons hostage by deliberately using obtuse subject headings and making Dewey Decimal numbers so long that people have to actually write them down to remember them, my desk is directly under the air conditioning vent, the fact that mistakes made in cataloging are not life-threatening, terrifying reference librarians with our knowledge of M.A.R.C., M.E.S.H., A.A.C.R.2, L.C.R.I., O.C.L.C., and P.R.I.S.M., staying off my feet all day, cataloger parties, and eccentricity is not only allowed but expected

WHAT CATALOGERS DISLIKE
ABOUT BEING CATALOGERS

Low pay, reference librarians who treat us like pond scum, waiting for the Library of Congress to make needed changes in subject headings, reference librarians who blame us for past cataloging errors we had nothing to do with, authors with two last names, confusing title pages, serials that change titles, eye strain and carpal tunnel syndrome, priority of rules over judgment, being viewed as the Antichrist by computer-phobic patrons who regard the demise of the card catalog as intellectual homicide, reference librarians who hold us responsible for absurd L.C. subject headings, working in a basement, wasting my talents on the trash ordered by reference librarians, having a reference librarian tell me that every three books is a "rush," having our work constantly critiqued by reference librarians who know nothing about cataloging, reference librarians whose lack of knowledge of M.A.R.C. prevents them from adequately serving the user, reference librarians who browse through and borrow books from the cataloging room before they've been cataloged, reference librarians who refer to us as "support staff," children's librarians who buy odd formats

CATALOGER FANTASIES

Waking up one morning to find that elves had eliminated my backlog and cleaned up my dirty database, being given a ton of money by a national grocery store chain to rearrange all their stock in logical order, meeting the cataloger of my dreams at an A.L.A. annual meeting, serving as the technical advisor for a t.v. sitcom based in a cataloging room, achieving agreement among librarians that the inventory control portions of descriptive cataloging are not worth the cost, finding a current name heading for the singer who used to be called Prince, cataloging with a computer that responds to voice commands, entering the 50 millionth record onto O.C.L.C., creating serial cataloging records for all Frederick's of Hollywood and Victoria's Secret sales brochures, taking a time machine to the month after barcoding is completed, pulling the plug on all bibliographic utilities and watching reference librarians try to cope, being given complete freedom to straighten out everything I think is wrong with L.C. subject headings, cataloging the music library of the Klingon Planetary Archives, discovering a previously undocumented incunabula, having Paul Newman jump down out of the READ poster in my office and into my lap

SUBJECT HEADINGS THAT CATALOGERS WOULD LIKE TO SEE L.C. ADOPT

Limbaugh, Rush—suicide.

PIGS (Instead of "Swine"); LIGHT BULBS (Instead of "Electric Lamps, Incandescent"); MADONNA—UNDERWEAR—PURCHASING; UNCOMBABLE HAIR SYNDROME; MOVIES (Instead of "Moving Pictures"); STALKING; GILLIGAN'S ISLAND—MAPS; BODICE—RIPPERS; POTBOILERS; JERKS; DUCK DETECTIVES; MENSTRUAL CRAMPS (Instead of "Dysmenorrhea"); CATS—SUPERIORITY OVER DOGS; LIMBAUGH, RUSH—SUICIDE; FACTS, UNTRUE; BED-WETTING (Instead of "Enuresis")

GOOFY SUBJECT HEADINGS

God — video recordings.

BABOONS — CONGRESSES; SEPARATED PEOPLE; FUZZY LOGIC; LOST ARCHITECTURE; FINGER SPELLING; SPONTANEOUS COMBUSTION, HUMAN; LADYBUGS — RELIGIOUS ASPECTS; ONE LEG RESTING POSITION; ANOREXIA — COOKBOOKS; CANARIES — SEX MANUALS; SKIN DISEASES — ATLASES; POTATO ART; BOOPS; BOOPS-BOOPS; HUMAN — PLANT RELATION-SHIPS; LEATHER CONTESTS; ORGASMS — TEXAS; BEACH NOURISHMENT; NARCISSISTIC INJURIES; YO-YOS (TOYS, NOT PEOPLE); BILL, BUFFALO; SAUCE, BATTLE OF THE; POSTHUMOUS MARRIAGES; IMAGINARY CONVER-SATIONS; DOG, C. FRED; GOD — VIDEO RECORDINGS; HAMLET — ENGLISH TRANSLATIONS; DINOSAUR SOUNDS — AUDIO RECORDINGS; TELEPHONE SIGN LANGUAGE; CHURCH WORK WITH COWGIRLS

WORST PERSONAL HABITS

Picking and biting my cuticles, not cleaning my coffee cup for months at a time, looking into my neighbor's bedroom window at night, watching "Baywatch" on t.v. every week, straightening up other people's desks, correcting people who use "less" instead of "fewer," being overly indulgent of my cat's personal habits, wearing too much purple, speaking in "M.A.R.C." rather than English to reference librarians I despise, taking my shoes off at work, yelling at people when I have P.M.S., snooping through people's desks for candy, emitting audible flatulence at work after lunch, stealing lunches from the staff refrigerator, eating cough drops at my desk for the sole purpose of violating the "no food in offices" rule in my library, scratching in public, turning down corners on pages instead of using a bookmark, insisting that the toilet paper in the staff bathroom feed from the top, flossing once a year right before my annual dental check-up, neglecting the dust balls under my sofa, purposefully misshelving key reference books to bug the reference librarians, whistling while I catalog, refusing cataloging input from reference librarians, constantly putting off the cataloging of weird children's formats, expecting perfection from everyone, even reference librarians

PET PEEVES OF CATALOGERS

People who make fun of catalogers, people who cut in line, people who are late, bad drivers who

1) tailgate,

2) do not use turn signals,

3) park illegally in handicapped spaces,

4) approach Formula One speeds on interstate straightaways,

5) circle parking lots looking for a closer spot,

6) equip their cars with radar detectors,

7) park in fire lanes,

8) drive slowly in the left lane,

9) use two parking spaces,

10) park at a different angle than everyone else,

smokers, litterers, dogs, people who own dogs, unruly children, parents who leave their unruly children unattended in public places, people who abuse the English language, people who are assholes, people who pop plastic bubble package liners, telephone solicitors, people who don't take their yard sale signs down after the sale, people who wear beeping watches, husbands who boast about being great cooks but who never clean the kitchen, people who leave long phone messages, people who decorate for Christmas before Thanksgiving, people who hyphenate "anal retentive," men who wear their slacks so low that you are forced to look at their butt crack, people who leave the toilet seat wet, people who talk at plays, concerts, operas, and movies, bi-metal tuna cans that cannot be flattened, people who leave their drawers (furniture) open, people who leave their drawers (underwear) open

TOP FIVE PEOPLE
CATALOGERS ADMIRE

1) ELEANOR ROOSEVELT
2) MOTHER THERESA
3) MICHAEL GORMAN (editor in chief of *AACR2*)
4) SANFORD BERMAN (author of *The Joy of Cataloging*)
5) LORENA BOBBITT

EPITAPHS CATALOGERS WANT
ON THEIR TOMBSTONES

"I TOLD YOU I WAS SICK"

"OUT OF BODY, BACK IN FIVE"

"DUST"

"THE QUEEN OF O.C.L.C."

"SHE KNEW THE RULES"

"SHE WAS FUN TO BE AROUND
EVEN IF SHE WAS A CATALOGER"

"HE WAS JUST VISITING THIS PLANET"

"I WON'T BE IN ON MONDAY!"

"SHE GOT RID OF THE BACKLOG"

"FOR HOLDING SEE MAIN ENTRY"

"LOGGED OFF"

Chapter 14

HOW TO TELL
IF YOUR KID
WILL GROW UP
TO BE A CATALOGER

Many parents have asked themselves, "How do I know if my kid will grow up to be a cataloger?" Yes, in today's polyglot, multi-cultural world the collective gene pool continues to expand and diversify. You may think that you are a perfectly normal reference librarian and that there is absolutely no chance that your kid will grow up to be a cataloger, but don't be so sure. They're putting some funny chemicals into the drinking water these days. And if you're a cataloger, the reverse is also true. Prepare yourself for the day when Johnny comes home from school and suddenly declares that he wants to be a doctor, a lawyer, or even, God forbid, a reference librarian. Actually there are some early warning signs that can tip you off to your child's genetic orientation. Does your child have that elusive quality of catalogerness? Read the pages ahead to find out.

You know your kid will be a cataloger if he collects Mattel cataloger action figures.

You know your kid will be a cataloger if he enjoys staying in on sunny days and creating authority control files.

You know your kid will be a cataloger if she chastises you for folding a page in your book to mark your spot.

You know your kid will be a cataloger if he subscribes to *Catalogers Illustrated*.

You know your kid will be a cataloger if she enjoys finding mistakes in the local library's catalog.

You know your kid will be a cataloger if she wallpapers her room with old catalog cards.

Chapter 15

YOU MIGHT BE
A CATALOGER
IF . . .

You dress like this.

The mid-life crisis has become accepted as an inevitable stage in the growth and development of post-modern Americans. What exactly is the mid-life crisis? It is that sinking feeling you get in your mid 40s that your biological clock is winding down and if you're ever going to fulfill your human destiny you better get started now. Put another way, it's that tumultuous period when married people suddenly divorce, straight people suddenly declare themselves gay, and chimney sweepers suddenly go to library school to become catalogers. Yes, cataloging is a profession that many people don't get into until after they've tried something else. How can you tell if this is going to happen to you? Read the pages ahead and check out the warning signs.

You might be a cataloger if the first thing you do when you visit your daughter-in-law is check the lint basket in the dryer to make sure it is clean.

You might be a cataloger if you can actually program your v.c.r.

You might be a cataloger if you go to Cancun for your vacation and end up spending all your time studying the Mayan ruins.

You might be a cataloger if you always go grocery shopping with a calculator.

You might be a cataloger if you tip the table dancer at a bachelor party and tell her to "take this money and go to library school."

You might be a cataloger if you give motivational tapes instead of money to street panhandlers.

Index